Peter Brook

Born in London in 1925, Peter Brook attended Magdalen College, Oxford, and by 1946 was already directing in Stratford (*Love's Labour's Lost*) and London (*Huis Clos*). The fifty or so remarkable productions which followed include Anouilh's *Ring Round the Moon* with Paul Scofield and Whiting's *A Penny for a Song* (1951), *Titus Andronicus* with Olivier and Brook's own music and designs (1955), T.S. Eliot's *The Family Reunion* and Arthur Miller's *A View from the Bridge* (1956), the musical *Irma la Douce* and Dürrenmatt's *The Visit* (1958), *King Lear* with Scofield (1962), *The Physicists* in London and *Serjeant Musgrave's Dance* in Paris (1963), Peter Weiss's *Marat/Sade* (1964), *US* (1966), Seneca's *Oedipus* with Gielgud for the National (1968) and *A Midsummer Night's Dream* for the RSC (1970).

After founding what is now called the Centre International de Créations Théâtrales at the Bouffes du Nord in Paris, Brook mounted *Orghast* in Iran in 1971, a tour of Africa in 1972 – out of which evolved *The Conference of the Birds* – *Timon of Athens* in 1974, *The Ik* (1975), *Ubu* (1977), *The Cherry Orchard* (1981) and *The Mahabharata* (1985). His more recent theatre work includes *The Man Who, Qui est là?*, Beckett's *Oh les beaux jours!*, *Le Costume* and *The Tragedy of Hamlet*

Among his opera productions are *The Marriage of Figaro* and *Boris Godunov* at Covent Garden and *Faust* and *Eugene Onegin* at the Met. His films include *Moderato Cantabile* (1960), *Lord of the Flies* (1963), *King Lear* (1970), *Meetings with Remarkable Men* (1979) and *The Mahabharata* (1989). His first book, *The Empty Space*, appeared in 1968, and he has since published *The Shifting Point* (1987), *There are No Secrets* (1993), *The Open Door: Thoughts on Acting and Theatre* and his autobiography *Threads of Time* (1998).

Also in the Dramatic Contexts series

Peter Brook

*E*voking
(and *F*orgetting)
*S*hakespeare

Nick Hern Books
London
www.nickhernbooks.co.uk

A Nick Hern Book

Evoking Shakespeare was first published as a paperback original
in Great Britain in 1998 by Nick Hern Books Limited,
14 Larden Road, London W3 7ST

Reprinted 1999, 2000, 2001

This expanded edition, re-titled *Evoking (and Forgetting)
Shakespeare*, first published in 2002

A CIP catalogue record for this book is available from
the British Library

ISBN 1 85459 712 4

Typeset by Country Setting, Kingsdown, Kent CT14 8ES
Printed and bound in Great Britain by Biddles of Guildford

Evoking Shakespeare

*Y*ou pick up a newspaper – you think it's today's paper – and you read it with interest. Then suddenly you realise that this is yesterday's paper, and it's of no interest at all. Why is this? The men and women who put the paper together are undoubtedly intelligent, they write well, yet what they have written is ninety per cent dead the next day and the newspaper is only good to wrap up fish. What then is the difference between a page of yesterday's paper and a page of Shakespeare written hundreds of years ago? Why is Shakespeare not out of date? This sounds like a frivolous, easy question. But in fact, if you think of it, the easy answers can't satisfy any of us. Because what would be the easy answer? For instance, 'Shakespeare was a genius.' What understanding can we get from the word 'a genius'? Or else, 'Shakespeare was a great man of his time.' What does that help us to understand? Or else, to take the answers that the contemporary school of criticism might give: 'Shakespeare was more interested in going to bed with a boy than with a woman.' Does that in any way open up to us the true mystery of the phenomenon of Shakespeare? You will all remember that not so long ago people were seriously trying to discover whether Shakespeare really existed, and there were many theories over the last hundred years which put other names in the place of 'Shakespeare' – Bacon, Marlowe, Oxford, etc. The absurdity of this is that, again, it doesn't help us. You change the name, that's all. The mystery remains . . .

I went to Russia recently, and somebody stood up in an audience and said: 'We all know here that Shakespeare came from Uzbekistan because the name "Sheik" is an Arab term and a "peer" is a wise man, so "Shakespeare" was a code name to tell everyone that he was a Crypto-Moslem living in a Protestant country where Catholics were being persecuted.' Again, does this help us to enter into the Shakespeare enigma? Was Chekhov a Czech? There was another snobbish, racist view that was current for a long time in England, which held that as Shakespeare came from the country and was a poor boy who went to the local school, he was incapable of reaching the level of education that his plays reveal. In fact I think he was about twenty-eight when he wrote his first play. If you think of the capacity for assimilation of words, of impressions, of all the young people today who are making films at the age of twenty and twenty-one, if you think that Shakespeare was living in a period when there was a coming and going across London of people from all parts of the world, there is one thing that one can, I think, assume as a fact. That is that to be able to write his plays, Shakespeare must have had an extraordinary memory. Let us start from here.

*U*ndoubtedly, Shakespeare was genetically endowed with an extraordinary capacity to observe, an extraordinary capacity to assimilate and an extraordinary capacity to remember. I was talking about this the other day with a young conductor, about the possibility, even when one is very young, to record in one's brain a complex score. It's clear that that was one of Shakespeare's extraordinary capacities.

*D*on't forget that he lived in a very, very active and busy city which was London at the time, where it was sufficient to go into any bar to hear conversations between people who had crossed the seas from all parts of the world. So his ears absorbed an extraordinary variety of information. Genetically speaking, Shakespeare was a phenomenon, and the bald head we have seen on so many pictures had an amazing, computer-like capacity for registering and processing a tremendously rich variety of impressions. This is the Shakespeare brain,

the Shakespeare instrument, and it is also,
I think, our starting point. Now, is it sufficient
to say he had a great memory? I don't think
so. For even if he could allow impressions
to enter into his brain in all their richness,
in all their complexity, that still would not be
enough to make of him Shakespeare the unique
dramatist. So, we are forced to conclude that
another fundamental characteristic was there
in him. We could call it 'creativity'. But even
then where does that word lead us, what does
it explain? Let's be very simple. We can say
he was a poet and nobody can contradict us –
because, after all, he wrote poetry. However,
being a poet comes from somewhere. What,
in fact, in concrete terms, is the ground out
of which this particular thing called 'poetry'
arises? A feeling for words, yes – a love of
literary expression, yes, but that is not enough.
We are looking for something very very
fundamental.

*W*hat is fundamental is that a poet is a
human being like every one of us – with

a difference. The difference is that we, at any given moment, don't have access to the whole of our lives. Just look at ourselves now. At this very moment, as we are sitting here together. None of us is capable of penetrating below the conscious level of his or her listening, to enter into the entire richness of what we have absorbed over our whole life. In many of us, it could take a long search to dig into our past impressions. For some of us it would even need years with a psychiatrist to reach into those strange tunnels where all one's experiences are buried waiting to be revived. But a poet is different. The absolute characteristic of 'being a poet' is the capacity to see connections where, normally, connections are not obvious.

T. S. Eliot describes this in relation to coffee spoons – 'I've measured out my life in coffee spoons'. The coffee spoon at one and the same time evokes the human associations that are personal to the poet, and which also reach out far beyond the personal. Now let's return to Shakespeare and stay very close to indisputable facts. When Shakespeare wrote his plays, we have every reason to believe that he wrote fast. He was a practical man, who was writing in a practical theatre for productions that had to go on constantly; and, if you look at his output and the amount of years that it covers, he must have written at great speed. We've got no reason to believe that he was the sort of author who wrote a draft, put it away, then twenty years later took it out of his drawer and reworked it. Everything suggests that there weren't drafts; there's no record of drafts of Shakespeare's plays being found, nor of manuscripts that were not used. Everything suggests the opposite — that the most extraordinary of his plays were written in the heat of the moment, with a burning passion to put down exactly what he was imagining.

*H*e always began to write a play with a story. And here, I think, we can see the differences between the writer in the newspaper — the

good writer in the Morgenpost – and
Shakespeare. If you are writing the story of a
crime for a newspaper, you write in a concise
way, you write on one level, you only describe
the surface of the action. Shakespeare had the
greatest respect for story-telling, but he did
something totally different. At each second
he was conscious not only of the action
itself but also of the relationships on an
infinite number of levels that were connected
to that action. So he was forced to develop
for himself a very extraordinary and complex
instrument which we call 'poetry', by which
within one single line he could give both the
narrative meaning – which has to be there,
the human character meaning which has to be
there – and at the same time find the appro-
priate words amongst the twenty thousand
English words that were at his disposal: find
the words that contain the resonances, that
bring together all the different levels of
association that he was carrying within him.

*T*hen there is another aspect to this phenomenon. A play of Shakespeare's is not longer than any ordinary play, a paragraph of the text is the same length as the ordinary paragraph in today's newspaper; but the density – the density of the moment – is where the whole interest for us lies. This density involves many elements, and one of the most important is the imagery: but there are also the words, and then the words take on extraordinary dimensions through the fact that the words are not just 'concepts'.

*E*ven if a concept is something necessary in speech, it is a tragically pathetic portion of the amazing whole that speech can offer. Concept is that little thin intellectual strain that the whole of western civilisation has bowed down to excessively for so many centuries. Concept is there, but beyond concept is the 'concept brought into life by image', and beyond concept and image is music – and word music is the expression of

what cannot be caught in conceptual speech.
Human experience that cannot be concep-
tualized is expressed through music. Poetry
comes out of this, because in poetry you have
an infinitely subtle relationship between
rhythm, tone, vibration and energy, which give
to each word as it is spoken concept, image
and at the same time an infinitely powerful
further dimension which comes from sound,
from the verbal music. And yet, I think how
dangerous it is even to mention the word
'music'. This can lead to a terrifying mis-
understanding. An actor can take this to
mean, 'Ah! I have a musical voice so I can
speak musically'. Let's be clear. Word music
in the poetic sense is something very subtle;
word rhythm is something very subtle; but
tragically in theatre schools all over the world
this has been reduced to a set of rules. If
actors are taught that Shakespeare wrote in
pentameters, and the pentameters have a
certain beat, and the actors try to use this
in their speech, you get a dry, empty music,
which is not the living music that is there in
the words.

So let's come back to the central questions.
What is the life within these plays? What,
in fact, is the Shakespeare phenomenon?
Shakespeare wrote, I think, thirty-seven plays.
Within these plays, there must have been
about a thousand characters. That means that
in his plays Shakespeare himself – about whom
we know so little – did something unique in
the history of all writing. He managed moment
after moment to enter into at least one
thousand shifting points of view. So now it
must be clear that the moment one tries to
reduce Shakespeare in any way to any single
viewpoint one is doing oneself a great dis-
service. If you say Shakespeare was a fascist –
indeed there are books on the subject which
say 'Shakespeare was a fascist', and there are
productions of *Coriolanus* to prove that
Shakespeare hated the people and was a fascist
– or else *The Merchant of Venice* shows that
Shakespeare was anti-semitic – all these
narrow-minded misunderstandings are based
on seizing one portion of one play and
saying: 'Ah, now we know why the play was

written.' The result of this approach today is above all sexual: we witness every sort of sexual interpretation of a play in attempts to prove that the play was written to reveal this or that sexual hidden relationship. Take a step back and look more broadly, more generously, and you see that Shakespeare has equal compassion and equal identification with all these shifting and changing attitudes, and he puts them all the time one in front of the other. At that point you find that it is almost impossible to discover a Shakespeare point of view, unless you say that being Shakespeare he contained in himself at least a thousand Shakespeares. But why is this important for us to understand?

Consider the form of theatre that Shakespeare entered into. It was already very exciting and vibrant – the Elizabethan playhouse had the same excitement as the cinema had twenty to thirty years ago – the cinema in which Orson Welles made *Citizen Kane* was a cinema in which a whole new world of possibilities was opened. Now this

new form of theatre was a theatre that was
based on a platform – roughly like this one
where I am standing – on which imagery
could come and go. As there was no scenery,
if someone said, 'We are in a forest', we were
in a forest, and the next second if they said,
'We are not in the forest', the forest had
vanished. That technique is faster than a cut
in the cinema. In a film, you have the total
picture of a forest – cut – to a total picture
of, say, Berlin; but these are two separate
things. When this is evoked by an actor with
words it's much quicker, because the actor, as
he is saying 'forest', can, within the same line
of verse, make the forest – and Berlin – and
you and me – appear – disappear – show you
already a big close-up of a face, go into a
heart, and the forest can reappear and go away
again. This fluidity is beyond any form of
film technique that's yet been invented.

*T*he architecture of the playhouse helped
this greatly. Shakespeare's platform was a
structure with different levels. There was a

level up here, and there was still another level
higher up that was used from time to time.
And now as I talk I realise that I am about to
say something that terrifies people today here
in Berlin. I don't know if I dare to mention
the word which, when I used it here about ten
years ago, sent a feeling of horror through the
entire audience. The word was 'metaphysical'.
Ten years ago in the political climate of Berlin,
the only thing that mattered was a strict
political point of view on this and that, and
anything that went beyond that was weak and
old-fashioned and soft at the edges. You must
tell me whether times change, whether the
word 'metaphysics' is less poisonous and
dangerous. But you can be certain that for
Shakespeare and for his audience, and for the
time in which he was living, with the tremendous mixture of people in transformation,
with ideas exploding and collapsing, there was
a lack of complete security. This was a blessing
because it created a very deep intuitive sense
that behind this chaos there was some strange
possibility of understanding, related to another
sort of order, an order that had nothing to do

with political order. That meaning is present through all the plays of Shakespeare, and – as Gordon Craig wrote a hundred years ago – if one refuses to accept the reality of a world of spirits it's much better to burn all the works of Shakespeare because they don't have any meaning at all any more. Shakespeare's theatre was a meeting-place between audience and players, in which scenes of life could be seen with great intensity, second by second.

*E*very visible dimension was accompanied by its invisible dimension, and that's why the action took place horizontally and vertically throughout all Shakespeare's plays. Now one can begin to see how it is that his form of writing had to be so compact and so dense. Also, I think one can see something else if one makes, just for a moment, this obvious relationship between his stage and today's cinema. Not because there was a freedom to have big scenes and small scenes, and battle scenes and spectacles – that's obvious. Something quite different. I don't know if it's ever struck you as strongly as it's always struck me that the cinema has developed a very, very complex artificial language which everyone can understand. One minute you have a long shot, next minute you have a close shot, next you are somewhere else, and this very complex syntax is crystal-clear all over the world to people of every culture, every background, and one can say every level of education. Gordon Craig, whom I knew when he was about ninety, said to me: 'I can't go to the cinema.' I said: 'Why not?' 'When I am sitting there', he said, 'and one minute I am looking at the picture of a mountain, then suddenly it jumps and there is a big face right in front of me, I can't understand anything at all.'

Now he — Gordon Craig — was unique and his points of view were always eccentric, but he expressed truly what a strange language the cinema was developing. However, he was alone in his reaction, and almost all the entire rest of humanity without difficulty followed long

shot, cut, close shot, cut, tracking shot, as
a simple and natural language. Now, in the
Elizabethan theatre, exactly the same thing
happened with poetry. An extremely complicated form evolved itself in which at one
moment somebody is speaking to someone
else in a natural everyday way, and yet, two
words later, they are using expressions that
you would never, ever, use in a normal conver-
sation. And he wrote strange adjectives, and
used sudden jolts in rhythm that could never
occur in life. Or within the phrases suddenly
there is a philosophical inquiry, a metaphysical
riddle that could never appear between two
people chatting together. Now from one point
of view this is an artificial language, an
artificial language for connoisseurs, but for
the Elizabethan audience there was no
problem: as for filmgoers today, it seemed
completely natural – natural because it was
necessary. The audience sitting there was not
composed of intellectuals saying: 'Ah, this is
a triumph of style', or arguing: 'What is the
stylistic reason behind this?'

When Shakespeare's plays were put on for the big popular audience, we have no evidence to suggest that anyone found this unfolding structure of words in any way unusual. It was many hundred years before someone would begin to say: 'Ah, I love going to the theatre, because I love its "artificiality".' 'Artificiality' only entered the theatre after Shakespeare's time, with scenery, make-up, *trompe l'oeil*, *chiaroscuro*, and then what are called 'theatre lovers' began to say: 'I love the artificiality of the stage.' But in fact, in Shakespeare's open arena, with the people standing around a platform, everything, whether natural or unnatural, seemed just like life.

When Shakespeare wrote: 'I am holding a mirror – we hold a mirror up to nature' – what this implies is that human beings within human life are being reflected. But that doesn't mean that they are reflected naturalistically, like in real life, not even artificially. When on my way here I saw a sign saying 'Kultur ist

heute', the word 'Kultur' filled me with horror
because 'Kultur' can easily lead one to believe:
'If it's artificial – ah, then it's culture!' No.
A true mirror of life is never cultural, never
artificial, it reflects what is there. And a theatre
does not only show the surface, it shows what
is hidden behind the surface, in the intricate
social interrelations of the people and, behind
that, what is the ultimate existential meaning
of this activity called life – all of these go
together, and are shown in the great mirror.
But to show the whole of life in this way is
an incredible task, and it demands a form
that is extraordinarily compact which is why
I come back to the same point. Moment by
moment the material is of such enormous
density that it demands every resource that
language has to offer. This means poetry. Not
poetry as prettiness but poetry as compact-
ness, poetry as language charged with intensity.

*L*et's now come back to our real difficulty,
to the present. Today we see that if we try to
stage a play of Shakespeare, the challenge is to

help the audience to look and listen with the eyes and ears of the present. What we look at must seem natural now, today. 'Seem natural' means that we don't put into question what we see. If you once think, 'Is this natural or unnatural?' you're kaputt. An actor is speaking and taking a glass of water, this is natural, and at that moment that person goes into poetry, into very complex speech – that must also seem natural – and if they do a strange movement, that must be natural too. In other words, the problem is adapting this material to the present moment, the present moment being now – the moment when people are sitting here in the audience.

*B*ut there's a trap. 'The present' and 'contemporary' are not the same thing. A director can take any play of Shakespeare and can make it contemporary in the simplest, crudest way. For instance, you can have people coming on stage with guns and riding motorbikes, and they shit on stage. There are a hundred ways in which you can bring something into the

recognisable present. As a director you are
free, but this freedom brings you unavoidably
against a tough and painful question. It obliges
you to be deeply respectful, sensitive and
open as you explore the text. You have to ask
yourself as director: are you in touch with all
the levels of the writing which are rich, fruitful
and meaningful and life-giving as much today
as in the past, or are you saying either
I haven't noticed these levels, or they are not
interesting, or just I don't care? You can do
what you want — but one must recognise
the gap between a crude modernising of a
text and the amazing potential within it that
is being ignored. And as there are so few
potentials in the theatre of this quality, then
one must recognise that one is taking a risk
which perhaps is not worth taking. To sum
up. The article in yesterday's newspaper has
only one dimension and it fades fast. Each line
in Shakespeare is an atom. The energy that
can be released is infinite — if we can split it
open.

Q *It seems that you work in Paris of your own free will and that usually means, as with* Qui est là, *that you are doing Shakespeare in French. How many of these levels that you've been describing actually suffer in working with Shakespeare in a foreign language or are there some advantages to that?*

A very interesting question, because the plays don't suffer, but I do. For an Englishman it is a real suffering. Because the moment you translate, one level of the music goes. What is extraordinary about Shakespeare is that there is so much in his plays that even when you take away what with most poetic writers would be ninety per cent of their true value, an extraordinary and magnificent material remains. With Shakespeare the mysterious power is there even in translation, out of which comes the energy that can lead to performance. It is there in the characters, in their relations, in all the other aspects, and also in the ideas that are within his language —

all of that leaves something tremendous even when this magical level of the words is diminished. And of course it's very interesting in exchange to work with translators and to see – for instance in French – the problem is very interesting, because in French you have the language which is perhaps the farthest removed from English, it's a completely different way of thought and way of expression.

*A*nd a complicated phrase with strange adjectives, which seems completely natural in English, if it is translated very faithfully into French, becomes extraordinarily artificial, pompous and flowery. So the French translator has to make a choice and simplify the line to rediscover its purity, at the expense of sacrificing some of what in English is part of its real value.

Q *Is there a special way in which
Shakespeare is dealing with violence,
destruction, negative aspects of life,
and is this way still concerning us?*

I have just been working on a play of Beckett
and the same question is always asked. Is he
pessimistic, is he optimistic, should we be
pessimistic, should we be optimistic today?
And, you see, these are all politicians' lies.
Optimism in front of reality is a lie, pessim-
ism is a masturbation and a self-indulgence.
But the third attitude is extraordinarily
difficult because it means opening oneself to
what is intolerable in human existence and
what, on the contrary, is radiant in human
existence — simultaneously. Now, the reason,
when some years ago we spent a long time
working on the *Mahabharata*, was that the
Mahabharata is about war, about violence,
about all the themes that are in the present-
day cinema. And at the same time the deepest
meaning of conflict in the human pattern is
explored in a way that is very different from a

film about the horror of war. It can lead us into feeling more alive rather than more suicidal, and I think that this really is the quality that you find in Greek tragedy, where the worse the events, the truer you know them to be. And yet the truer you know them to be the more inevitable you see them to be, and the more the reaction for yourself in an audience is neither complacent, nor suicidal. Curiously, this intensifies your capacity to live. And this seems to me present in the whole work of Shakespeare. For instance, you take *King Lear*. Nowhere in *King Lear* can you find anyone closing their eyes to the cruelty of mankind, and yet the play is not a black existentialist play showing that mankind is a worthless species, nor a naive expression that all mankind is noble and beautiful. The vertical and the horizontal are there at one and the same time to be grasped if one wants to and if one can.

Q *Why do you relate this capacity — memory — of Shakespeare to his genes?*

I think — perhaps you don't agree — that a prodigious memory and a capacity to listen and observe are part of the inborn qualities of a human being. And what is interesting is to see the use that's made of them. And there one can see that Shakespeare, from his first play to his last, lived very actively and very intensively with his own life experiences. The potential was obviously there when he was born and when he first put pen to paper, with his first play. But at the moment when he wrote his first play he hadn't lived the human experiences and the human interrogations that led him later to be able to write *Hamlet*, and write *King Lear*, and eventually to write *The Tempest*. So that one sees a very interesting relationship between what's inborn and what is developed by life.

Q   *What can one understand in* Hamlet *in relation to a metaphysical level?*

I think that in *Hamlet*, perhaps of all plays, this is very simple, because if you take the ghost out of *Hamlet* it's no longer the same story. If you take the spirits out of the *Midsummer Night's Dream*, it's no longer the same story. You can make other stories about a man killed by his brother or a son becoming suspicious and deciding to revenge himself on his uncle — but that's not *Hamlet*. In *Hamlet* the shock that is brought to a young man is because he actually sees his father's ghost, and through the father's ghost he learns that the father has been murdered. One of the questions that run through the play is: 'Is this an illusion?' The word 'illusion' is there from the start. Is this an illusion or is this a reality? Now, one doesn't have to go further than that to see that somebody who is tormented by that question is forced to enquire into every aspect of life. He questions his relations with women, he doubts the purity of a woman who at the same time seems crystal-clear and totally honest. What does this mean? Is this mysterious figure saying, 'You must kill' an authority to be respected or not? These are not simple questions, but they are all brought into existence by the spirit, in a way that in the *Midsummer Night's Dream* the whole question of love becomes concrete because of an interplay between physical love and other levels incarnated by spirits. And the same goes for *The Tempest*: I wrote down this morning something which I think is interesting because it touches on this question of the different levels of Shakespeare. These are the last words of *The Tempest*, maybe the last words Shakespeare ever wrote. And it's interesting if one listens to them, from the point of view of an actor who is trying to understand what in fact the character of Prospero could be.

> *My ending is despair*
> *Unless it be relieved by prayer*
> *Which pierces so that it assaults*
> *Mercy itself and frees all faults.*
> *As you from crimes would pardon'd be*
> *Let your indulgence set me free.*

It's interesting for us to look at this in detail because within this one can see both the possibilities and the difficulties that are there all through Shakespeare's works.

The first phrase is very simple and introduces a theme that everyone can understand on its first level:

> *My ending is despair*
> *Unless it be relieved by prayer*

But if you take it in isolation, the thought is banal. Listen: despair and prayer rhyme. In any little English boarding house you could see this written on the wall on a little card saying, 'My ending is despair unless it is relieved by prayer.' If the actor says it like a homely motto, he is ignoring the fact that the word is not 'by prayer' but 'by prayer which' and 'which' is a moment of suspense. What follows the 'which'?

> *Which pierces so that it assaults*
> *Mercy itself*

Next comes 'assaults', and you can always see in Shakespeare's writing that, as he writes,

when his hand comes back to the beginning
of a new line there is always a special force.
You feel it in the actual texture of the writing
of his verse that the end of a phrase is like an
upbeat in music that's leading to – what? –
suspense. And the word that follows is
'mercy'. Now can we understand a prayer that
not only 'penetrates' but also can 'assault'
mercy? So the idea of assault is extraordinary
– there is a power in the words themselves,
they are very unusual words – 'I assault
mercy.' A prayer assaults mercy. There is
something tremendously powerful not only in
the words but in the image, the image of
something abstract and vast called mercy
being assaulted like a citadel.

I am trying to open up for you the fact that
we are in front of something, which we
cannot ever finally understand. Now this is
very important, because the whole of work in
Shakespeare production and Shakespeare
acting turns around the question of when you
have the right to be absolutely sure and when,

on the contrary, your only true position is one
of open questioning. I don't know if we have
any cardinals or high theological authorities
in the audience today, but personally I don't
believe that there is a theological authority
today who can tell us with absolute certainty
what it means to say: 'a prayer which pierces
so that it assaults mercy.' I think this is
deliberately written by a poet not to encap-
sulate an understanding but to open a burning
mystery. And you see that it carries on by
saying that if that incomprehensible act
happens, it leads to freedom.

> *and frees all faults.*
> *As you from crimes would pardon'd be*

— very strong word 'crimes' —

> *Let your indulgence set me free.*

So if you now look at this incredible complexity of writing, written — I am sure — in
the heat of the moment, you can draw out
of this a chain, and the chain is: despair —
prayer — assault — mercy — crime — pardon —
indulgence — free. If an actor or if a director

take this to be just a happy ending you can
say they haven't bothered to listen to the words.

*I*f you think in terms of clichés and decide
that Shakespeare wrote the play just as a piece
about colonialism, then you are refusing to
see that what leads to the last word 'free'
concerns the meaning of freedom in all its
dimensions and implications.

*N*one of the words we just quoted stands in
isolation. The passage leads inexorably to the
last word of all, and the questions it evokes
are truly for today wherever they are spoken.
Always the closer one comes in contact with
the Shakespearean material, the more this is
a meeting point between living material and
ourselves and is never just the expression of
his point of view. And the words only come
into new life when once again they become
the meeting point with people of today,
whether they are actors, directors or spec-
tators. With the purpose of leaving us in

front of open questions which we must struggle with once again – for ourselves.

*A*fter which I must quote Shakespeare and ask you with your indulgence to set me free.

Berlin, 12 May 1996

Forgetting Shakespeare

My first memories of Shakespeare were of rolling sounds, of actors playing with passion and little attempt at meaning. Then came the great Stratford revolution. Meaning came first, discussed, analysed and put into practice by intelligent minds: playing verse became a clean and honest craft. With the new school, the old familiar lines were shown to be shrewd, crisp and full of sense. A mould was broken. Soon, however, a new problem arose as actors began to confuse verse with everyday speech, thinking that talking 'as in life' was all that was needed. As a result, with haphazard, insensitive phrasing and false stresses the verse became lame and ordinary, the plays

lost their passion and their mystery and
jealous writers questioned whether
Shakespeare was really so much better than
themselves.

So the scholars reacted firmly and put all
the weight on the technical differences
between verse and prose, insisting on the
form being respected. This led to a new
heresy called 'presenting the text' or 'sharing
the text with the audience'. Many a young
actor was led to believe that in front of
great words he was a sort of newsreader
and that his primary function was to let
the lines be heard and speak for themselves.
From this came the worst of all horrors,
the 'Shakespeare' voice.

All these approaches have now worn themselves out. Today, we must recognize a different challenge in front of a new danger.
There is a subtle poison that invades much of
our social life – it is called 'reductionism'.

In practice, this means reduce the dimensions of whatever is unknown and mysterious: debunk wherever possible, cut everything down to size. In this way, young actors are once more drawn into the trap of believing that their own everyday experience can give them what they need and that they can base their understanding on their personal set of references. This leads him – or her – to apply current political and social clichés to situations and characters whose true riches go far beyond ideas. When for instance one tries to use *The Tempest* to illustrate stereo-typed notions about slavery, domination and colonialism, or to play complex characters to fit in with sexual attitudes that happen to be in the air, the result is taking characters who have fascinated audiences over the century because of their being so unfamiliar, so hard to encompass – and making them ordinary.

*H*amlet was well aware of this when he cried out:

*You would play on me. You would seem
to know my stops. You would pluck out the
heart of my mystery . . .*

So what can one say to a young actor about
to tackle one of these great roles? Forget
Shakespeare. Forget that there ever was such
a man. Forget that these plays had an author.
Remember only that your responsibility as an
actor is to bring human beings to life. So just
assume, as a trick to help you, that the character you are preparing to play really existed.

*I*magine that Hamlet really existed, imagine
that someone followed him secretly wherever he went with a tape recorder, so that
the words he spoke were really his own.
Where does this lead to? The consequences
of such an attitude go very far.

*F*irst of all, all temptation to think that
'Hamlet' is 'like me' is swept away. Hamlet
is only interesting because he is not like

41

anyone else, he is unique. To prove this to
yourself, do an improvisation of any part of
the play you choose. Listen honestly to your
own off-the-cuff, very personal material, it
may be very interesting but word after word,
line after line, has it the sustained potency
of Hamlet's speech? You will agree that this
is not very likely. And it is clearly ridiculous
to imagine that in situation after situation,
matching Ophelia with the girl one loves,
or Gertrude with one's own mother, one can
express oneself with Hamlet's intensity, his
vocabulary, his humour, such richness of
thought. This leads to realizing that only
once in history did such a person as Hamlet
exist, live, breathe and talk. And we have
him on tape! The tape is the witness that
these words were really spoken. Thanks to
this belief, we begin to long passionately
to know such an unusual person. Does it
then help us to think at the same time of
Shakespeare, the author? To analyse his
intentions, the influences on him of his
time, etc? To examine his verse techniques,
his methods, his philosophy? However

fascinating this may be, does it help? Or
does it help more simply, more directly to
approach the play in the way that Irish
actors work on Irish plays? In the best Irish
plays, the words are never ordinary, they seem
like 'fine writing' but, as Synge suggested,
the author is as it were lying on the floor in
the attic, listening to real speech, unique
real speech, coming up to him through a
crack in the ceiling below. In Synge, O'Casey,
Friel, the Irish reality expresses itself in
prose that is poetry. If we choose, we can
even count the syllables on our fingers,
but, if we do so, will this help to make our
playing more truthful? The Irish actor and
actress simply sense that the person they
are playing is real and as they accept that
richness of musical utterance is natural
to the character, it rises with equal fluency
to the tongue of the performer. The actor's
task is not to think of words as part of a
text, but of words as part of a person whom
we believe actually minted them in the heat
of the moment.

*T*oday, actors on television and in films are often amazingly true-to-life when they play reconstructions of actual events. In the theatre, actors playing for instance the police interrogation of some victim of police brutality, using material drawn from authentic recordings and transcripts have no intellectual confusion. If the person they are trying to bring to life uses an unexpected word, a strange phrase, a striking metaphor or even a repellent image, the actor is not confused by asking what 'the author' meant, nor what the author's 'period' was dictating to him. But, the moment the challenge is playing Shakespeare everything gets muddled. Turning half towards the author, half towards the character is a double-think. Double thinking wastes energy and concentration.

*S*uppose we were to overhear Lear saying to Cordelia:

> *And take upon 's the mystery of things*
> *As if we were God's spies.*

In our new game, we pretend that Lear actually said this spontaneously, which is far more amazing than if we think that it was carefully worked out by a man at a desk with pen and paper. Then we are compelled to ask ourselves what sort of man could – off-the-cuff, when being led away to prison after a cruel and violent battle – improvise such words? We feel a need to know what extraordinary experiences had made up his life, what moments of deep self-searching, what special sensitivity could have given this apparently tyrannical king such a dense and fervent inner activity. We see that a psychological approach is inadequate, a textual approach is insufficient and anything that cuts Lear down to size or makes him 'like someone else' is useless. Our way into the character must be through recognizing that the words he uses show us who he is.

*A*n actor for instance who has pondered merely on Lear's actions may come to the conclusion that anyone who gives his kingdom to his daughters is an old fool. He is

forced to reconsider this when he realizes
that a man who in this extreme situation
instead of self-pity can reflect on 'things'
and their 'mystery' and who can in one
compact two-word expression link 'God'
to 'spy' has no commonplace mind; there is
no trace of dotage in such thinking. So who
is he? The question plunges actors beyond
Freud, beyond Jung, beyond reductionism.

*T*his does not lead us to sloppiness, to less
concern for the fine detail of the verse. On
the contrary, every syllable takes on a new
importance, each new letter can become a
vital clue in reconstructing a highly complex
brain. We can no longer start with an idea,
a concept, nor a theory of the character. There
are no short cuts. The entire play becomes
one great mosaic and we approach the music,
the rhythms, the strangeness of the images,
the alliteration, even the rhymes, with the
surprise and awe of discovery, because they
are necessary expressions of the inner
patterns of exceptional human creatures.

*S*hakespeare never intended anyone to study Shakespeare. It is no accident that he made himself so anonymous.

*I*t is only when we forget Shakespeare that we can begin to find him.

Paris, 28 September 1994